EMMANUEL JOSEPH

The Leader's Mic, Public Speaking, Action, and the Psychology of Inspiring Teams

Copyright © 2025 by Emmanuel Joseph

All rights reserved. No part of this publication may be reproduced, stored or transmitted in any form or by any means, electronic, mechanical, photocopying, recording, scanning, or otherwise without written permission from the publisher. It is illegal to copy this book, post it to a website, or distribute it by any other means without permission.

First edition

This book was professionally typeset on Reedsy. Find out more at reedsy.com

Contents

1. Chapter 1: The Essence of Leadership Communication — 1
2. Chapter 2: The Power of Storytelling — 3
3. Chapter 3: The Psychology of Persuasion — 5
4. Chapter 4: Crafting a Compelling Message — 7
5. Chapter 5: The Role of Body Language — 9
6. Chapter 6: Overcoming Public Speaking Anxiety — 11
7. Chapter 7: Engaging Your Audience — 13
8. Chapter 8: The Art of Active Listening — 15
9. Chapter 9: Inspiring Action Through Vision — 17
10. Chapter 10: Building a Culture of Open Communication — 19
11. Chapter 11: Handling Difficult Conversations — 21
12. Chapter 12: The Impact of Emotional Intelligence — 23
13. Chapter 13: Leading by Example — 25
14. Chapter 14: Communicating Change — 27
15. Chapter 15: The Role of Feedback in Growth — 29
16. Chapter 16: The Future of Leadership Communication — 31
17. Chapter 17: The Legacy of a Leader — 33

1

Chapter 1: The Essence of Leadership Communication

Leadership is not just about making decisions or giving orders; it's about conveying vision and values through effective communication. The first step is understanding your audience, knowing their motivations, fears, and aspirations. By connecting on an emotional level, a leader can foster trust and loyalty, which are essential for a cohesive team. This chapter explores the foundations of impactful leadership communication.

Effective leadership communication starts with clarity. A leader must articulate their vision and goals in a way that is easily understood by all team members. This involves breaking down complex ideas into simple, relatable concepts and using language that resonates with the audience. Clarity ensures that everyone is on the same page and working towards the same objectives.

In addition to clarity, consistency is crucial. A leader's message should remain consistent across all channels of communication, whether it's a team meeting, an email, or a public speech. Consistency reinforces the leader's vision and values, making it easier for team members to align their actions with the overall goals. It also helps in building trust, as it shows that the leader is reliable and steadfast.

Finally, authenticity is key to effective leadership communication. A leader must be genuine in their interactions, showing empathy and understanding. This builds a strong connection with the team, making them more likely to be motivated and inspired. Authenticity also involves being transparent about challenges and setbacks, which fosters a culture of openness and collaboration.

2

Chapter 2: The Power of Storytelling

Stories have been a part of human culture for millennia, serving as a powerful tool for conveying complex ideas and emotions. A leader who can tell compelling stories can inspire, motivate, and unite a team. This chapter delves into the elements of a great story and how leaders can use narratives to drive action and change within their organizations.

A well-crafted story captures the audience's attention and keeps them engaged. It starts with a relatable protagonist, often the team or organization itself, facing a challenge or opportunity. The narrative unfolds with a series of events that build tension and anticipation, leading to a resolution that aligns with the leader's vision. This structure not only entertains but also reinforces the key message in a memorable way.

Emotional resonance is another critical element of powerful storytelling. A story that evokes emotions such as hope, fear, joy, or empathy creates a deep connection with the audience. Leaders can achieve this by highlighting personal experiences, real-life examples, or hypothetical scenarios that reflect the values and aspirations of the team. Emotional stories are more likely to be remembered and acted upon.

Furthermore, stories can simplify complex ideas and make them more accessible. By framing abstract concepts in a narrative context, leaders can help their team members understand and relate to the message. For instance, explaining a new strategy through the story of a previous successful project can make the concept more tangible and less intimidating.

Lastly, storytelling can foster a sense of shared identity and purpose. When team members see themselves as part of a larger narrative, they are more likely to feel a sense of belonging and commitment. Leaders can use stories to celebrate achievements, acknowledge challenges, and envision a future where everyone plays a crucial role. This collective narrative strengthens the team's cohesion and drives them towards common goals.

3

Chapter 3: The Psychology of Persuasion

Understanding the psychological principles behind persuasion can make a significant difference in a leader's effectiveness. This chapter examines techniques such as reciprocity, authority, and social proof, providing practical examples of how these principles can be applied in leadership scenarios to influence and motivate team members.

Reciprocity is a powerful principle that leverages the human tendency to return favors. When leaders show genuine appreciation, offer help, or provide resources, team members feel compelled to reciprocate by contributing their best efforts. This creates a positive cycle of mutual support and collaboration, enhancing overall team performance.

Authority is another key factor in persuasion. Leaders who demonstrate expertise, confidence, and credibility are more likely to be trusted and followed. This involves not only having the necessary knowledge and skills but also communicating them effectively. Leaders can establish authority by sharing insights, making informed decisions, and consistently delivering results.

Social proof is the concept that people are influenced by the actions and opinions of others. Leaders can harness this principle by highlighting examples of successful team members, sharing positive testimonials, or showcasing collective achievements. When individuals see their peers embracing a certain behavior or mindset, they are more likely to follow suit, creating a culture of excellence.

Additionally, the principle of scarcity can be a motivating factor. When resources, opportunities, or rewards are perceived as limited, team members are more likely to value and pursue them. Leaders can strategically communicate the significance and uniqueness of certain initiatives or goals, encouraging a sense of urgency and commitment. However, this should be done ethically, ensuring that the scarcity is genuine and not manipulative.

4

Chapter 4: Crafting a Compelling Message

A leader's message must be clear, concise, and compelling. This chapter explores the art of message crafting, focusing on the importance of clarity and consistency. We'll discuss how to identify the core message, structure it effectively, and deliver it in a way that resonates with the audience, ensuring it is memorable and actionable.

The first step in crafting a compelling message is identifying the core message. This involves distilling the main idea or objective into a simple, powerful statement. The core message should capture the essence of what the leader wants to convey and why it matters. It serves as the foundation for all subsequent communication and helps in maintaining focus and coherence.

Once the core message is identified, structuring it effectively is crucial. A well-structured message follows a logical flow, with a clear beginning, middle, and end. The introduction should grab the audience's attention and set the context. The body should provide supporting information, evidence, or examples that reinforce the core message. The conclusion should summarize the key points and provide a clear call to action or takeaway.

In addition to structure, delivery is a vital aspect of message crafting. The way a message is delivered can significantly impact its reception and effectiveness. Leaders should consider the tone, language, and medium that best suit their audience. For example, a motivational speech may require a passionate and energetic tone, while a strategic plan may need a more formal and analytical approach. Adaptability and audience awareness are key to successful delivery.

Finally, ensuring that the message is memorable and actionable is essential. Leaders can use techniques such as repetition, metaphors, and anecdotes to make the message stick. Repetition reinforces the core message and helps it to be remembered. Metaphors and anecdotes create vivid imagery and emotional connections, making the message more relatable and impactful. Additionally, providing clear and specific actions or next steps ensures that the audience knows exactly what to do and how to contribute to the leader's vision.

5

Chapter 5: The Role of Body Language

Nonverbal communication can often speak louder than words. This chapter highlights the significance of body language in public speaking and leadership. From eye contact to posture, we'll uncover the subtle cues that can enhance or undermine a leader's message. Practical tips on using body language to convey confidence and authority will be provided.

Eye contact is a powerful tool for building connection and trust with an audience. When leaders maintain eye contact, they project confidence and sincerity, making it easier for the audience to engage with the message. However, it's important to strike a balance—too much eye contact can be intimidating, while too little can make the speaker seem disinterested. The key is to make genuine, intermittent eye contact with different members of the audience.

Posture and gestures also play a crucial role in effective communication. A strong, upright posture conveys confidence and authority, while slouching can signal disinterest or insecurity. Gestures should be purposeful and natural, complementing the verbal message rather than distracting from it. Open and expansive gestures can make the speaker appear more approachable and engaging.

Facial expressions are another important aspect of body language. A leader's facial expressions should match the tone and content of their message.

Smiling can create a sense of warmth and approachability, while a serious expression can convey gravity and importance. Leaders should be mindful of their facial expressions to ensure they are reinforcing their message and not sending mixed signals.

Lastly, the use of space can influence how a message is perceived. Moving around the stage or room can create a dynamic and engaging presentation, while remaining stationary can make the speaker appear rigid or uninspired. However, excessive movement can be distracting, so it's important to find a balance. By using space effectively, leaders can create a sense of energy and engagement that captivates their audience.

6

Chapter 6: Overcoming Public Speaking Anxiety

Even seasoned leaders can experience anxiety before speaking in public. This chapter offers strategies for managing and overcoming public speaking anxiety. Techniques such as deep breathing, visualization, and mindfulness will be explored, along with practical advice on preparing for and delivering a confident and composed speech.

Deep breathing is a simple yet effective technique for calming nerves before a speech. By taking slow, deep breaths, speakers can reduce physical tension and lower their heart rate, creating a sense of relaxation and control. Practicing deep breathing exercises regularly can help build this skill and make it easier to use during high-pressure situations.

Visualization is another powerful tool for managing public speaking anxiety. This involves imagining a successful presentation, visualizing oneself speaking confidently and engagingly, and receiving positive feedback from the audience. By mentally rehearsing a positive outcome, speakers can boost their confidence and reduce anxiety.

Mindfulness practices, such as meditation and grounding exercises, can also help manage anxiety. By staying present in the moment and focusing on the task at hand, speakers can prevent their minds from wandering to negative thoughts or outcomes. Simple mindfulness techniques, such as focusing on one's breath or noticing physical sensations, can be effective in reducing anxiety.

Preparation is key to overcoming public speaking anxiety. Thoroughly researching and rehearsing the speech can help build confidence and reduce uncertainty. Practicing in front of a mirror, recording oneself, or presenting to a small group of trusted friends or colleagues can provide valuable feedback and help the speaker feel more comfortable and prepared. Additionally, having a clear outline or notes can serve as a helpful guide during the presentation.

7

Chapter 7: Engaging Your Audience

An engaged audience is more likely to be receptive and motivated. This chapter discusses techniques for capturing and maintaining audience engagement, including the use of humor, interactive elements, and rhetorical questions. We'll also explore the importance of adapting your presentation style to fit the audience's preferences and expectations.

Humor is a powerful tool for capturing attention and making a presentation more enjoyable. When used appropriately, humor can break the ice, create a positive atmosphere, and make the speaker more relatable. It's important to use humor that is relevant to the topic and respectful of the audience to avoid misunderstandings or offending anyone.

Interactive elements, such as polls, questions, or activities, can keep the audience engaged and involved. By encouraging participation, speakers can create a more dynamic and engaging presentation. Interactive elements can also help reinforce key points and provide opportunities for the audience to apply what they have learned.

Rhetorical questions are another effective technique for engaging the audience. By posing thought-provoking questions, speakers can encourage the audience to think critically and reflect on the topic. Rhetorical questions can also create a sense of curiosity and anticipation, keeping the audience interested and invested in the presentation.

Adapting the presentation style to fit the audience's preferences and expectations is crucial for maintaining engagement. This involves understanding the audience's background, interests, and needs, and tailoring the content and delivery accordingly. For example, a technical audience may appreciate detailed data and analysis, while a general audience may prefer more relatable examples and anecdotes. By being flexible and responsive, speakers can ensure that their message resonates with the audience.

8

Chapter 8: The Art of Active Listening

Leadership communication is not just about speaking; it's also about listening. This chapter emphasizes the importance of active listening in building trust and understanding within a team. We'll discuss techniques for becoming a better listener, such as paraphrasing, asking open-ended questions, and providing constructive feedback.

Active listening involves fully focusing on the speaker, understanding their message, and responding thoughtfully. This requires more than just hearing the words; it involves paying attention to nonverbal cues, emotions, and underlying meanings. By practicing active listening, leaders can build stronger connections and foster a sense of trust and respect within their team.

Paraphrasing is a useful technique for demonstrating active listening. By summarizing the speaker's message in one's own words, the listener shows that they have understood and are engaged in the conversation. Paraphrasing also provides an opportunity to clarify any misunderstandings and ensure that both parties are on the same page.

Asking open-ended questions encourages deeper conversation and allows the speaker to elaborate on their thoughts and feelings. Open-ended questions cannot be answered with a simple "yes" or "no"; they require more detailed responses, which can lead to richer and more meaningful discussions. This technique also shows that the listener is genuinely interested in understanding the speaker's perspective.

Providing constructive feedback is an essential aspect of active listening. Feedback should be specific, actionable, and delivered in a supportive manner. It should focus on behaviors and outcomes rather than personal traits, and it should be framed in a way that encourages growth and improvement. By providing thoughtful feedback, leaders can help their team members develop their skills and reach their full potential.

9

Chapter 9: Inspiring Action Through Vision

A leader's vision is a powerful motivator for action. This chapter explores how to articulate a clear and inspiring vision that resonates with the team. We'll discuss the importance of aligning the vision with the team's values and goals, and how to communicate it in a way that inspires commitment and action.

Articulating a clear vision involves painting a vivid picture of the future that the team can strive towards. This vision should be ambitious yet achievable, providing a sense of purpose and direction. Leaders should use descriptive language and relatable examples to make the vision tangible and compelling. By clearly outlining what success looks like, leaders can motivate their team to take action and work towards a common goal.

Aligning the vision with the team's values and goals is crucial for gaining buy-in and commitment. Leaders should ensure that the vision reflects the team's core values and addresses their needs and aspirations. This involves seeking input from team members and incorporating their perspectives into the vision. When team members see how the vision aligns with their own values and goals, they are more likely to be motivated and engaged.

Effective communication is key to inspiring action through vision. Leaders should consistently communicate the vision through various channels and reinforce it in their daily interactions. This includes sharing stories, celebrating milestones, and recognizing contributions that align with the vision. By keeping the vision top of mind, leaders can create a sense of urgency and excitement that drives action and progress.

Lastly, leaders should provide clear and actionable steps for achieving the vision. This involves breaking down the vision into smaller, manageable goals and outlining specific actions that team members can take. By providing a roadmap and clear expectations, leaders can empower their team to take initiative and make progress towards the vision.

10

Chapter 10: Building a Culture of Open Communication

Creating a culture of open communication is essential for a high-performing team. This chapter discusses strategies for fostering an environment where team members feel comfortable sharing ideas, feedback, and concerns. We'll explore the role of transparency, inclusivity, and regular communication in building trust and collaboration.

Transparency is a cornerstone of open communication. Leaders should be open and honest about the team's goals, challenges, and progress. This involves sharing relevant information, being transparent about decision-making processes, and acknowledging both successes and setbacks. Transparency builds trust and ensures that team members feel informed and included.

Inclusivity is another key factor in fostering open communication. Leaders should actively seek input and feedback from all team members, regardless of their role or level of experience. This involves creating opportunities for team members to share their ideas, opinions, and concerns. By valuing diverse perspectives, leaders can create a more innovative and collaborative team environment.

Regular communication is essential for maintaining open communication. This involves establishing regular check-ins, team meetings, and feedback sessions. Leaders should encourage open dialogue, actively listen to team members, and address any concerns or issues promptly. Regular communication helps to build strong relationships and ensures that everyone is aligned and working towards common goals.

Leaders should also model open communication in their own behavior. This involves being approachable, actively listening, and providing constructive feedback. By demonstrating open communication, leaders set the tone for the team and encourage others to do the same. Creating a culture of open communication requires ongoing effort and commitment, but the benefits of increased trust, collaboration, and innovation are well worth it.

11

Chapter 11: Handling Difficult Conversations

Leaders often face challenging conversations, whether it's giving constructive feedback or addressing conflicts. This chapter provides practical guidance on navigating difficult conversations with empathy and professionalism. We'll discuss techniques for staying calm, being clear and direct, and finding solutions that benefit all parties involved.

Staying calm is essential for handling difficult conversations effectively. Leaders should manage their emotions and approach the conversation with a composed and rational mindset. This involves taking deep breaths, pausing to collect one's thoughts, and focusing on the issue at hand rather than personal feelings. Staying calm helps to create a more productive and respectful dialogue.

Being clear and direct is important for ensuring that the message is understood. Leaders should communicate their points clearly, using specific examples and avoiding vague language. It's important to address the issue directly and avoid beating around the bush. Clear and direct communication helps to prevent misunderstandings and ensures that everyone is on the same page.

Empathy plays a crucial role in difficult conversations. Leaders should show understanding and compassion for the other person's perspective and feelings. This involves actively listening, acknowledging their emotions, and validating their concerns. Empathy helps to build trust and rapport, making it easier to find mutually beneficial solutions.

Lastly, finding solutions that benefit all parties involved is key to resolving difficult conversations. Leaders should focus on identifying common goals and exploring potential solutions collaboratively. This involves being open to feedback, considering different perspectives, and seeking win-win outcomes. By working together to find solutions, leaders can address the issue while maintaining positive relationships and fostering a sense of teamwork.

12

Chapter 12: The Impact of Emotional Intelligence

Emotional intelligence is a critical skill for effective leadership. This chapter explores the components of emotional intelligence—self-awareness, self-regulation, motivation, empathy, and social skills—and how they contribute to effective communication and leadership. Practical tips for developing and applying emotional intelligence in leadership will be provided.

Self-awareness involves recognizing and understanding one's own emotions, strengths, and weaknesses. Leaders with high self-awareness are better able to manage their emotions and respond to situations effectively. This involves reflecting on one's actions and reactions, seeking feedback from others, and being mindful of how one's behavior impacts the team.

Self-regulation is the ability to manage and control one's emotions and impulses. Leaders with strong self-regulation remain calm and composed under pressure, making thoughtful and deliberate decisions. This involves practicing mindfulness, developing healthy coping mechanisms, and avoiding reactive or impulsive behavior. Self-regulation helps leaders maintain a positive and stable presence.

Motivation is the drive to achieve goals and pursue excellence. Leaders with high motivation are passionate about their work and inspire others to strive for greatness. This involves setting clear and challenging goals, maintaining a positive attitude, and persevering through setbacks. Motivated leaders create a sense of purpose and direction for their team.

Empathy is the ability to understand and share the feelings of others. Leaders with strong empathy build trust and rapport with their team, creating a supportive and inclusive environment. This involves actively listening, showing compassion, and considering the perspectives and needs of others. Empathy helps leaders connect with their team and address their concerns effectively.

Social skills are essential for building and maintaining positive relationships. Leaders with strong social skills excel in communication, collaboration, and conflict resolution. This involves being approachable, engaging in meaningful conversations, and fostering a sense of teamwork. Social skills help leaders build strong connections and create a cohesive and motivated team.

13

Chapter 13: Leading by Example

Actions speak louder than words, and leaders must lead by example to inspire their teams. This chapter discusses the importance of aligning actions with words and demonstrating the behaviors and values you want to see in your team. We'll explore the impact of authenticity, integrity, and consistency on leadership effectiveness.

Leading by example means embodying the values and behaviors that you expect from your team. This involves demonstrating commitment, accountability, and professionalism in your own actions. When leaders consistently align their actions with their words, they build trust and credibility, making it easier for the team to follow their lead.

Authenticity is a key component of leading by example. Leaders should be genuine and true to themselves, showing vulnerability and humility. This involves being honest about one's strengths and weaknesses, admitting mistakes, and seeking feedback. Authentic leaders create an environment where team members feel comfortable being themselves and taking risks.

Integrity is another critical aspect of leading by example. Leaders should uphold high ethical standards and act with honesty and fairness. This involves making decisions based on principles rather than convenience, treating others with respect, and standing up for what is right. Leaders with integrity inspire trust and loyalty from their team.

Consistency is essential for maintaining credibility and trust. Leaders should consistently demonstrate the values and behaviors they expect from their team, regardless of the circumstances. This involves being reliable, following through on commitments, and maintaining a steady presence. Consistent leaders create a stable and supportive environment where team members can thrive.

14

Chapter 14: Communicating Change

Change can be unsettling for teams, and effective communication is crucial during times of transition. This chapter offers strategies for communicating change in a way that minimizes resistance and fosters buy-in. We'll discuss the importance of transparency, addressing concerns, and providing a clear vision for the future.

Transparency is vital when communicating change. Leaders should be open and honest about the reasons for the change, the expected impact, and the steps involved in the transition. This helps to build trust and reduces uncertainty. Providing regular updates and maintaining an open-door policy for questions and concerns can further enhance transparency and keep the team informed.

Addressing concerns is another key aspect of communicating change. Leaders should actively listen to team members' concerns and provide clear and empathetic responses. This involves acknowledging their feelings, providing reassurance, and offering support. Addressing concerns helps to alleviate fears and fosters a sense of understanding and collaboration.

A clear vision for the future is essential for gaining buy-in and motivating the team during times of change. Leaders should articulate a compelling vision that highlights the benefits and opportunities of the change. This involves painting a positive picture of the future and explaining how the change aligns with the team's values and goals. A clear vision provides direction and inspires confidence and commitment.

In addition to transparency, addressing concerns, and providing a clear vision, leaders should also involve the team in the change process. This involves seeking input, involving team members in decision-making, and empowering them to take ownership of the change. By involving the team, leaders can create a sense of collaboration and shared responsibility, making the transition smoother and more successful.

15

Chapter 15: The Role of Feedback in Growth

Constructive feedback is essential for individual and team growth. This chapter explores the role of feedback in leadership, discussing how to give and receive feedback effectively. We'll provide practical tips for delivering feedback that is specific, actionable, and supportive, as well as creating a culture of continuous improvement.

Giving feedback effectively involves being specific and focused on behaviors rather than personal traits. Leaders should provide clear examples and explain the impact of the behavior on the team and the organization. This helps to ensure that the feedback is understood and provides a basis for improvement. Specific feedback is more actionable and helps team members know exactly what they need to work on.

Actionable feedback provides clear and realistic suggestions for improvement. Leaders should offer practical advice and resources to help team members develop their skills and achieve their goals. This involves setting clear expectations and providing ongoing support and guidance. Actionable feedback helps team members to see a clear path for growth and development.

Supportive feedback is delivered in a constructive and empathetic manner. Leaders should show understanding and appreciation for the team member's efforts and achievements. This involves using positive language, highlighting strengths, and offering encouragement. Supportive feedback helps to build confidence and motivation, making team members more receptive to suggestions for improvement.

Creating a culture of continuous improvement involves fostering an environment where feedback is valued and encouraged. Leaders should regularly seek and provide feedback, create opportunities for learning and development, and celebrate progress and achievements. This helps to create a culture of growth and excellence, where team members are motivated to continuously improve and reach their full potential.

16

Chapter 16: The Future of Leadership Communication

As technology and societal expectations evolve, so too must leadership communication. This chapter examines emerging trends and challenges in leadership communication, including the impact of digital communication tools, remote work, and diverse teams. We'll explore how leaders can adapt their communication strategies to stay effective in a rapidly changing world.

Digital communication tools have revolutionized the way leaders interact with their teams. Platforms such as video conferencing, instant messaging, and collaboration tools have made communication more efficient and accessible. However, they also present challenges, such as maintaining personal connections and managing information overload. Leaders must find a balance between leveraging technology and preserving the human element of communication.

Remote work has become increasingly common, presenting both opportunities and challenges for leadership communication. While remote work offers flexibility and autonomy, it also requires leaders to adapt their communication strategies to maintain engagement and collaboration. This involves establishing regular check-ins, using virtual team-building activities, and fostering a sense of community and belonging.

Diverse teams bring a wealth of perspectives and experiences, but they also require leaders to be culturally aware and inclusive in their communication. This involves understanding and respecting different communication styles, being mindful of language and cultural nuances, and creating an inclusive environment where everyone feels valued and heard. Leaders should embrace diversity as a strength and leverage it to drive innovation and creativity.

In addition to adapting to digital tools, remote work, and diverse teams, leaders must also stay attuned to changing societal expectations. This includes being transparent and accountable, promoting ethical and sustainable practices, and advocating for social justice and equality. By staying informed and responsive to these trends, leaders can build trust and credibility, and lead their teams with integrity and purpose.

17

Chapter 17: The Legacy of a Leader

A leader's impact extends beyond their tenure, leaving a lasting legacy. This chapter discusses the importance of reflecting on your leadership journey, celebrating successes, and learning from challenges. We'll explore how to create a positive and enduring legacy through effective communication, inspiring action, and fostering a culture of continuous growth and development.

Reflecting on your leadership journey involves taking the time to assess your achievements, challenges, and growth. This involves seeking feedback, acknowledging successes, and identifying areas for improvement. Reflection helps leaders gain insights into their leadership style and impact, and provides a basis for continuous learning and development.

Celebrating successes is an important aspect of creating a positive legacy. Leaders should recognize and celebrate the achievements of their team, both big and small. This involves acknowledging individual and collective contributions, expressing gratitude, and creating opportunities for celebration. Celebrating successes helps to build morale, motivation, and a sense of pride and accomplishment.

Learning from challenges is equally important for creating a lasting legacy. Leaders should embrace challenges as opportunities for growth and learning. This involves being open to feedback, taking responsibility for mistakes, and finding solutions for improvement. Learning from challenges helps leaders build resilience, adaptability, and continuous improvement.

Fostering a culture of continuous growth and development is key to creating a positive and enduring legacy. Leaders should invest in the development of their team, providing opportunities for learning, growth, and advancement. This involves creating a supportive and inclusive environment, promoting collaboration and innovation, and encouraging continuous improvement. By fostering a culture of growth, leaders can ensure that their impact extends beyond their tenure and leaves a lasting legacy.

The Leader's Mic: Public Speaking, Action, and the Psychology of Inspiring Teams

Description:

Unlock the art of leadership communication with "The Leader's Mic," a comprehensive guide that delves into the essential skills and strategies for inspiring and motivating teams through effective public speaking. This book explores the intersection of leadership, action, and psychology, providing practical insights and actionable techniques for leaders at all levels.

From understanding the foundations of impactful communication to mastering the power of storytelling and persuasion, "The Leader's Mic" covers a wide range of topics that are crucial for successful leadership. Learn how to craft compelling messages, use body language to convey confidence, and overcome public speaking anxiety with ease.

Dive into the psychology of persuasion and discover how to engage your audience, build trust through active listening, and inspire action with a clear and motivating vision. Explore the importance of open communication, handling difficult conversations with empathy, and leveraging emotional intelligence to connect with your team on a deeper level.

As you journey through the chapters, you'll gain insights into leading by example, communicating change effectively, and fostering a culture of continuous growth and development. The book also addresses the challenges of modern leadership, including digital communication, remote work, and diverse teams, providing strategies to adapt and thrive in an ever-evolving landscape.

"The Leader's Mic" is a valuable resource for anyone looking to enhance their leadership communication skills and create a positive, lasting impact on their team. Whether you're a seasoned leader or an emerging one, this book offers the tools and knowledge you need to inspire, motivate, and lead with confidence and integrity.